WIT~~HDRAWN~~

912540

DATE DUE

MAR 2 1 1995	OCT 2 1 199	JAN 2 0 2000	
OCT 5 199	NOV 5 1997	JUN 1 4 2000	
DEC 3 199	JAN 1 7 1998	JAN 2 4 2001	
FEB 7 1996	FEB 1 3 1998	MAR 0 0 2001	
OCT 17 199	MAR 4 1998	JAN 2 5 2002	
OCT 2 4 1996	NOV 2 4 1998	JAN 2 2002	
OCT 3 1 1996	DEC 2 1 1998		
FEB 2 0 1997	Jan.06		
5	JAN 2 0 1998		
MAR 1 4 199	MAR 4 1999		
SEP 2 9 1997	NOV 4 1999		

PRINTED IN CANADA

Okanagan College
Curriculum Resource Centre

EXPLORING
ELECTRICITY

Ed Catherall

Wayland

Exploring Science

Also in paperback:

Exploring Light
Exploring Magnets
Exploring Sound

Cover illustrations:
Above left *Electricity pylons in the USA.*
Below left *A circuit diagram, showing a battery, two bulbs and a switch.*
Right *An electric light bulb.*

Frontispiece *A powerpoint for recharging special batteries. The two red lights on the unit show that the recharger is working. Four batteries are in position.*

Editor: Elizabeth Spiers
Series Designer: Ross George

First published in 1989 by
Wayland (Publishers) Ltd
61 Western Road, Hove
East Sussex BN3 1JD, England

©Copyright 1989 Wayland (Publishers) Ltd

This edition published in 1991 by
Wayland (Publishers) Ltd

British Library Cataloguing in Publication Data
Catherall, Ed, 1931–
    Exploring electricity.
    1. Electricity
    I. Title   II. Series
    537

ISBN 0-7502-0266-1

Typeset by Direct Image Photosetting Ltd, Hove,
Sussex, England
Printed in Italy by G. Canale C.S.p.A., Turin
Bound in Belgium by Casterman S.A.

Contents

Static electricity 6

How is static electricity made? 8

Lightning 10

Detecting static charges 12

Electricity in your home 14

Dry-cell batteries 16

Circuits 18

Series circuits 20

Parallel circuits 22

Conductors and insulators 24

Electrical resistance 26

Heat from electricity 28

Light from electricity 30

Fuses 32

Water conducts electricity 34

Electroplating 36

Storing electricity 38

Electricity makes magnetism 40

Electric motors 42

Generating electricity 44

Glossary 46

Books to read 47

Index 48

STATIC ELECTRICITY

Left *Spectacular static electricity sparks, made when a steel ball is dropped into a high-energy electric field.*

A Van der Graaf generator. It can produce static electricity for experiments. The surface of the shiny metal hood collects the static charges.

When you undress, you can sometimes hear a crackling sound coming from your clothes. This is best heard if you are wearing nylon next to wool. If you undress in the dark, it is possible to see tiny sparks, like lightning, coming from your clothes. The sparks from your clothes are caused by static electricity and are best seen on dry days. You can sometimes feel the effect if you walk on thick nylon carpet and then touch a metal door handle. You can feel an 'electric shock' in your fingers.

The Ancient Greeks noticed that amber beads rubbing against fur or wool would attract dust and hairs. The Greek word for amber is *elektron,* which is where the word electricity comes from.

In the eighteenth century, the American Benjamin Franklin realized that static electricity is made of two static charges; he called them negative and positive. Negative charges are attracted to positive charges and try to reach them. When you hear your clothes crackling, your movements are causing the wool to rub against the nylon and this causes the nylon to be negatively charged. The wool becomes positively charged. When you undress and separate your clothes, the nylon's negative charges jump away to the wool, like lightning sparks.

ACTIVITY

YOU NEED

- **a plastic pen**
- **a plastic spoon**
- **a plastic comb**
- **a woollen cloth**
- **a cotton cloth**
- **a fur glove**
- **small torn pieces of newspaper**
- **a piece of rubber**
- **an iron nail**
- **a wooden ruler**

1 Tear the newspaper into very small pieces and put them on to a table.
2 Bring each item close to them. Does anything happen?

3 Rub the pen many times with the woollen cloth.

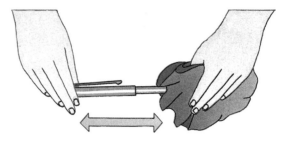

4 Bring the pen close to the paper. What happens? Is the pen charged with static electricity?
5 Rub the plastic spoon with fur.
6 Bring the spoon close to the paper. What happens?
7 Comb your hair with the plastic comb. Does the comb become charged?

8 Try rubbing the nail, the wooden ruler and the piece of rubber with the woollen cloth. Do these become charged with static electricity?
9 Try testing other materials.
10 Which material is easiest to charge?
11 Think of an experiment to prove this. Remember to make a fair test.

TEST YOURSELF

1. Where does electricity get its name from?
2. Describe how you would put a static charge on something.
3. Why do you sometimes hear a crackling sound when you undress?

HOW IS STATIC ELECTRICITY MADE?

Everything in the universe is made of tiny atoms. You are made of atoms; so are your table and chairs, the food that you eat and the air you breathe. Each atom is so tiny that it takes millions of them to form just one head of a pin.

Each atom contains charged particles. In the middle of each atom are the positively charged particles called protons, and neutrons – uncharged particles. Around the outside of each atom move the negatively charged particles called electrons. It is rather like the planets orbiting the Sun. You could consider the Sun as the protons and neutrons and the planets as the electrons.

Before an atom becomes charged with static electricity, the number of protons equals the number of electrons, so there is no charge. When wool and plastic are rubbed together, electrons can be made to move from one to the other. The atoms in the plastic pick up the electrons from the atoms in the wool. There are now too many electrons on the plastic, so it is no longer 'balanced' and is now negatively charged. The wool has lost electrons, so it is not 'balanced'; the protons make it positively charged. The wool and the plastic will attract each other. This is because unlike charges attract.

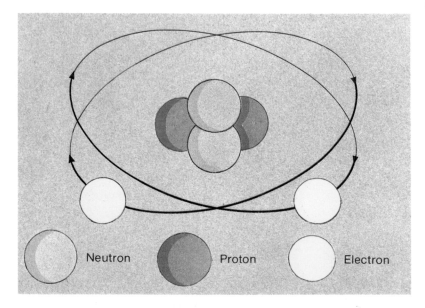

Neutron   Proton   Electron

Left A diagram of an atom, showing the electrons, protons and neutrons.

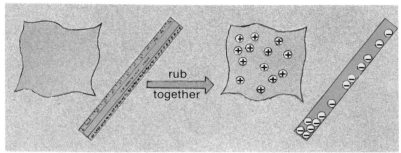

rub together

Left A diagram to show how static charge builds up when plastic and wool are rubbed together. The plastic takes electrons from the wool, leaving the plastic with a negative charge and the wool with a positive charge.

ACTIVITY

STATIC CHARGES

> YOU NEED
>
> - **a rubber balloon**
> - **a balloon inflator**
> - **a woollen cloth**
> - **thread**

1 Use the inflator to blow up the balloon.
2 Tie the neck of the balloon with thread.
3 Hold the balloon by the thread and ask a friend to rub the balloon gently with the woollen cloth. Do not rub too hard or fast, or the balloon will burst.

4 What happens when you bring a cloth close to the balloon?

5 Hold the charged balloon close to your friend's hair. What happens?

6 Place the balloon close to your nose. What can you feel?
7 Can you get a charged balloon to stick to the wall or under a table?
8 Hold your balloon above some dust or chalk dust. What happens?
9 Turn on a water tap until the water comes out as a thin stream.
10 Hold the charged balloon near to it. What happens?

TEST YOURSELF

1. Is an electron positively or negatively charged?
2. Draw an atom. Label the protons and electrons.
3. What happens to the electrons when you rub a rubber balloon with a woollen cloth?

LIGHTNING

You know that static electricity makes sparks when it jumps. Perhaps the most spectacular example of this is lightning. Sometimes, particularly if it is hot, heavy clouds become charged with static electricity. Positive charges tend to collect at the top of the cloud, while negative charges move to the bottom. Eventually, the charge builds up so much that the negative electrons jump. They are attempting to 'balance' themselves. When they jump, or discharge, the air around gets very hot. This is what causes the flash, and also makes a shock wave of pressure, which we hear as thunder.

There are two common types of lightning. Sheet lightning is where the charge leaps from one side of the cloud to another. Forked lightning is where the charge leaps to earth, sometimes branching out to other clouds on the way down.

These cloudbanks are producing sheet lightning (above) and forked lightning (below).

Forked lightning is very dangerous. If it hits anything, such as a tree, it will burn. If you are caught in a thunderstorm, never shelter under a tall tree, or a tree standing alone. Do not stand on high ground. It is quite safe inside a car or a building. Very high buildings have lightning conductors on them. These are strips of metal that take the static electricity safely down the outside of the building to the ground.

The thunder from the lightning flash is not dangerous. It can be used to find out roughly how far away the storm is. Sound travels much slower than light, so the noise of the thunder reaches you later than the flash. If there is a three-second gap between lightning and thunder, the storm is 1 km away.

ACTIVITY

POSITIVE AND NEGATIVE CHARGES

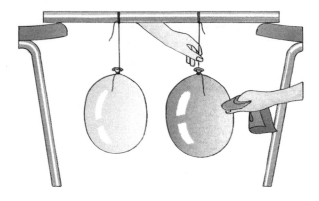

YOU NEED

- **2 rubber balloons**
- **a balloon inflator**
- **a broom handle suspended between 2 chairs**
- **thread**
- **2 empty plastic bottles**
- **a woollen cloth**

1 Use the inflator to blow up a balloon Tie thread around the neck.
2 Hang it from the broom handle.
3 Blow up the other balloon.
4 Suspend it from the broom handle near the other balloon.

5 Rub one balloon with the woollen cloth to charge it. How do the balloons react to each other?

6 Rub both balloons with the woollen cloth. You now have two negatively charged balloons. What happens?
7 Do like charges (i.e. the same charge) attract or repel (push away)?
8 Put 2 empty plastic bottles on a table.
9 Make sure that they do not roll.
10 Put them close together. What happens?

11 Rub one bottle with the woollen cloth. Place it near the other bottle. What happens?
12 Now rub both bottles with the woollen cloth.
13 What happens when you put the two bottles close together on the table?

TEST YOURSELF

1. What is lightning and how is it formed?
2. Why do you hear thunder after a lightning flash?
3. Which places should you avoid during a thunderstorm?

DETECTING STATIC CHARGES

You have found out that like charges repel each other and unlike charges attract each other (see page 8). Knowing this, it is easy to test whether a material is charged, by bringing it close to another charged material.

An instrument that detects static charge in this way is called an electroscope. There are all kinds, containing different materials as the charge indicator. One of the most popular is the gold-leaf electroscope. This has two charged strips of gold. When a like charge comes near, the leaves fly apart as they repel each other. If an unlike (opposite) charge comes near, the leaves move closer together. This is because the charge on the leaf and

the charge from the material are balancing one another.

It is best to use any sort of electroscope in dry air. If it is a moist day, the extra electrons leave negatively charged material and jump onto the water particles in the air. All the charge leaks away, and cannot be detected properly.

The two diagrams below show a gold-leaf electroscope: first, being approached by a rod carrying the same charge as the electroscope, and second, when the rod carries a different charge.

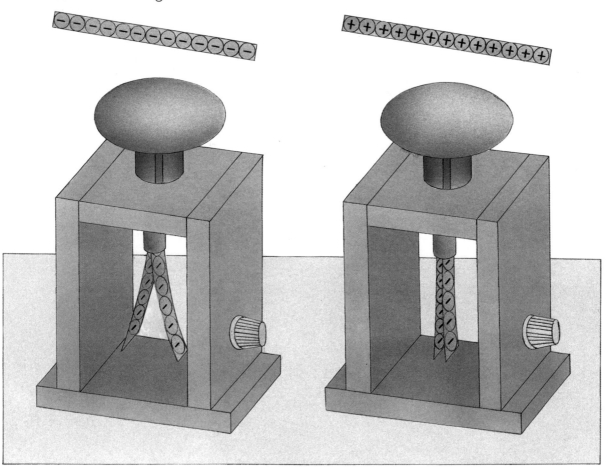

ACTIVITIES

MAKING A PAPER ELECTROSCOPE

YOU NEED

- **a long, thin strip of newspaper (60 cm × 5 cm)**
- **a wooden ruler**
- **a woollen cloth**
- **a plastic comb**
- **a plastic pen**

1 Fold the paper in half lengthwise.
2 Open it out and place it on a table.

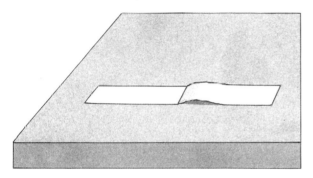

3 Stroke the paper with the woollen cloth.

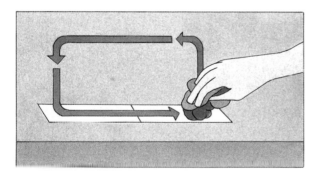

4 Pick up the paper with a ruler so that it hangs down over the ruler. What happens to the paper?

5 Rub the pen with the cloth. Hold the charged pen between the halves of the paper. What happens?

6 Are the charges on the paper and pen like or unlike?
7 Charge the comb. Hold it between the paper. What happens?
8 Are the charges like or unlike?

TEST YOURSELF

1. What is a static electricity detector called?
2. Why should you not attempt static experiments in wet weather?

ELECTRICITY IN YOUR HOME

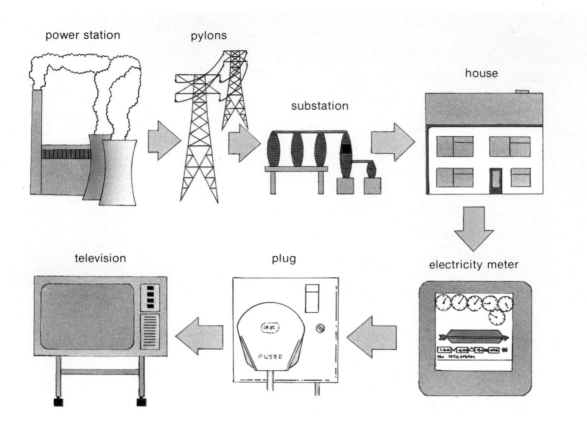

Static means to stay still. Static electricity charges stay still on a material. The charges can move only if they build up too high, such as in a thunderstorm. They jump away from the material; this is called a discharge.

This is not always the case. In some substances, such as metal, the electrons (negative charges) can flow like water. This is called current electricity. We can use wires to channel the electricity into machines to make them work.

Power stations create the current electricity that flows along wires until it reaches our homes. Before the electricity is used in the home, it flows through a meter. This records how much electricity your home has used. You must pay for the exact amount used. Electricity is a form of energy, so it can

This is the pathway of electricity that we use in our homes, places of work and in industry. Electricity is made in the power station and passes through a number of stages before it is used.

be changed into other types of energy. A great deal of the current electricity used in the home is changed into heat energy. The flowing electrons may be used to heat the element in an electric fire, an iron or hot water system. Electrical energy may be converted to light energy in a light bulb, or sound energy when a radio, cassette, disc player or television speaker is used. Mechanical (movement) energy can be made from the current. This is used to turn motors, as in a dishwasher, washing machine or electric drill.

ACTIVITY

READING THE METER

1 Ask someone where your electricity meter is.
2 Look at it. It will be one of two kinds: new-style digital display or old-style dial meter.
3 The digital display has a set of numbers. This is the meter reading. It will change as electricity is used in your home.

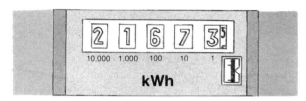

4 The old-style dial meter is easy to read once you know how! Look at the dials. There should be five of them.
5 Read the dials from left to right. There are examples to help you.

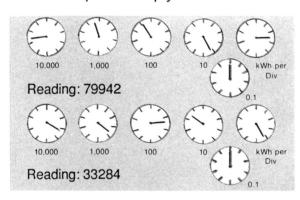

Reading: 79942

Reading: 33284

6 For either type of meter, look to find the wheel that turns when the electricity is switched on somewhere in your home. You will see a small part of it.

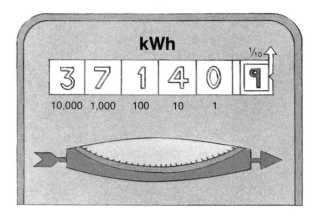

7 If possible, ask an adult to switch on different types of electrical equipment: something that heats up; gives sound; gives light; has a motor.
8 See how fast the wheel turns each time.
9 What sort of electrical equipment makes the wheel turn quickest? This is the most expensive.
10 Look at the meter reading every day. By how much has it changed?
11 Do this for several days.
12 Find out how much electricity your house uses each day. Is it roughly the same every day?
13 Are some days more expensive than others? If so, can you think of reasons why?

TEST YOURSELF

1. What is the difference between static and current electricity?
2. Name three electrical appliances (pieces of equipment) that convert electrical energy into heat energy.
3. Name three electrical appliances that convert electrical energy into mechanical energy.

DRY-CELL BATTERIES

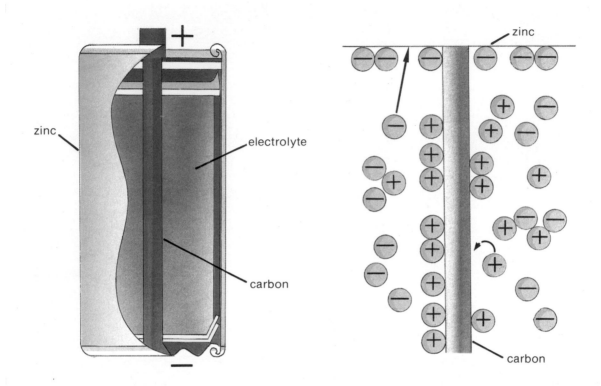

Two diagrams of a dry-cell battery. The diagram on the left shows the contents of the battery. The diagram on the right shows how the charges move to make an electric current.

You do not always use the mains electricity to power equipment in your home. It is very strong electricity, which can be inconvenient for small appliances, such as radios. It is also very dangerous. Mains electricity, incorrectly used, can kill. The best device to use in small pieces of equipment, and if you are doing electrical investigations like the ones in this book, is a dry-cell battery. You will be used to using these in flashlights, calculators and radios.

A battery turns chemical energy into electricity. Dry-cell batteries are not really dry, but contain a damp chemical paste called the electrolyte. This is made up of millions of positive and negative charges. The electrolyte is put into a battery case made of zinc. In the middle there is a carbon rod. This carbon rod often has a metal tip, which

makes a better connection to the equipment. The carbon rod and the zinc case are the electrodes of the battery. They are connected to the '+' and '−' terminals that you see outside the battery.

When a dry cell placed inside a flashlight is switched on, a chemical reaction starts in the paste which generates electric current. Electrons go to the zinc case and positive charges go to the carbon rod. The flow of electrons entering the flashlight's wires makes the bulb light up. When the electrolyte cannot react further the battery is dead and no more current will flow.

ACTIVITIES

1 Look at the shapes of the batteries. What do they have written on them?
2 What are their voltages? Where are the terminals?

3 If they are covered in thick paper, remove the paper to see the zinc case. What do you notice about the case?

> WARNING: if you try to open a battery to see inside, empty the contents on to thick layers of paper. Do not get the damp paste on your hands or clothes. It is a very strong chemical. Inside, there is only a black carbon rod and some dark grey paste. It is not worth the effort of looking inside!

MAKE YOUR OWN WEAK BATTERY

YOU NEED

- **a large, juicy lemon**
- **a large paper clip**
- **2 short pieces of insulated copper wire**
- **a 1.5 V bulb in a bulb holder**

2 Tightly wind one end of a piece of wire around the paper clip.
3 Stick the paper clip into the lemon.

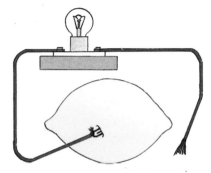

1 Uncover the ends of the wire.

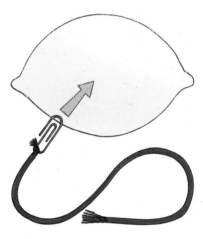

4 Fix the other end of the wire to the bulb holder.
5 Fix the other piece of wire to the other terminal of the bulb holder.

6 Push the other terminal of the wire deep into the lemon.

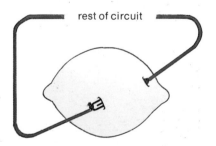

rest of circuit

7 Darken the room. Does the bulb glow?
8 Jiggle the wires in the lemon.

TEST YOURSELF

1. Explain why you must never play with household electricity.
2. Draw a dry-cell battery. Label the parts.

CIRCUITS

On page 17, you turned a lemon into a dry-cell battery and, to prove that you had made electricity, you used it to light a bulb. In a dry-cell battery, the electrons within the electrolyte cannot move until there is a pathway linking the zinc to the carbon electrode.

If you connect the zinc electrode to a bulb with a wire, then run another wire from the bulb to the carbon electrode, there is a path for the electrons to flow through. This path is called a circuit.

There are a lot of electrons at the zinc electrode (negative) and much fewer at the carbon terminal (positive). You know that unlike charges attract, so if there is a circuit for the electrons to flow along, they will move from negative to positive. To keep the flow going, the battery uses an electrical force called the voltage. This is the difference in charge between the two electrodes. This measurement is made in volts (V), named after Alessandro Volta, an Italian scientist who made the first electric cell or battery.

The current is measured in amperes or amps (A), named after the Frenchman A.M. Ampère.

A microscope photograph of a set of microchips (integrated circuits). These are tiny, complicated circuits containing many parts. They are found in many electrical devices, including computers. The microchip circuits are printed on to a wafer made of silicon.

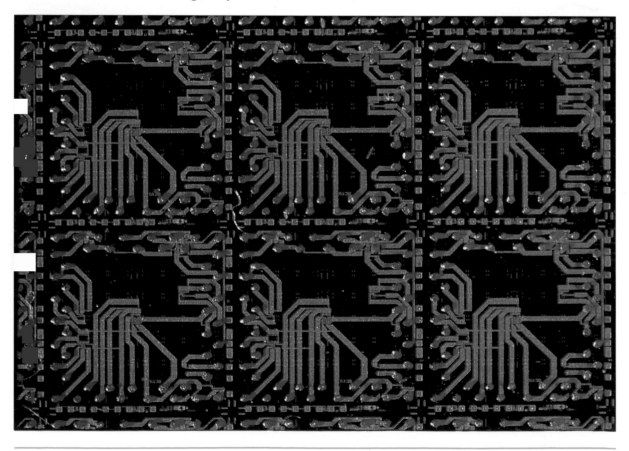

ACTIVITY

MAKING A SIMPLE CIRCUIT

> **YOU NEED**
>
> - **a dry-cell battery in a battery holder**
> - **a bulb in a bulb holder**
> - **2 crocodile terminal clips**
> - **a screwdriver**
> - **2 short lengths of insulated copper wire**

1 Check that the ends of the copper wires are uncovered.
2 Connect one crocodile clip to one end of a length of wire.
3 Connect the other end to one side of the bulb holder.
4 Fasten the crocodile clip to one battery terminal.

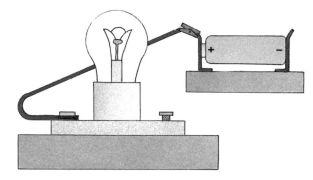

5 Notice that the bulb does not light up, as there is no circuit (pathway) for the electrons.

6 Now connect another crocodile clip to the other wire. Connect the other end of this wire to the other side of the bulb.
7 Fasten this crocodile clip to the other battery terminal.

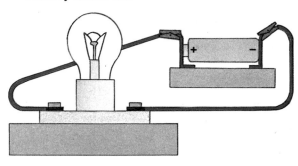

8 What happens? If your electrons can flow around your circuit from the zinc to the carbon, your bulb should light.
9 Disconnect one crocodile clip from the battery terminal.
10 What happens to the bulb? Why?
11 Swap the terminals. Does the battery still work?

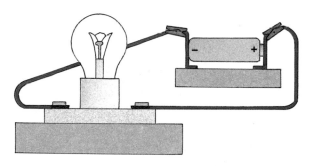

12 Draw your complete circuit with the bulb alight.

> WARNING: do not leave the bulb alight for long. You will waste both bulb and battery.

TEST YOURSELF

1. Why is a circuit necessary for electricity to flow?
2. Draw a simple circuit.
3. What is the difference between volts and amps?

SERIES CIRCUITS

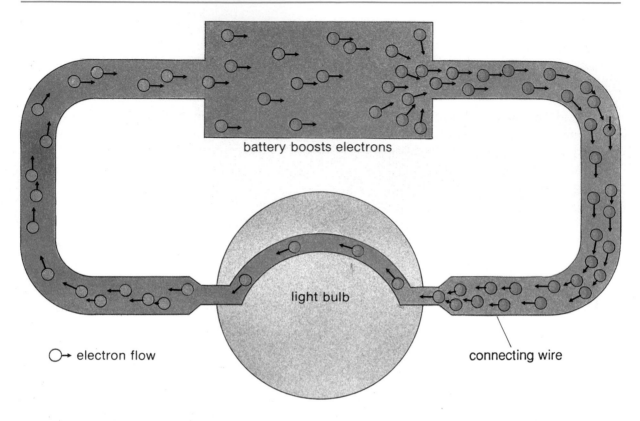

battery boosts electrons

light bulb

O→ electron flow

connecting wire

When an electric circuit is made, electrons flow from the negative terminal of the battery to the positive terminal. In order to see that the electric current is flowing, a bulb can be put in the circuit. Electrical energy is converted into light energy in the bulb.

A bulb is rather like a narrow bridge. The electrons are slowed down as they jostle to cross the bridge. This means that they have less energy to complete the circuit, when they are boosted again by the battery. We could put a second bulb in the circuit after the first bulb. The bulbs are placed one after another in a series. This is called a series circuit. The electrons now have two bridges to cross. They have twice the work to do. There are not enough electrons crossing both bridges to light both bulbs strongly, so the bulbs are dimmer than before.

Electron flow in a circuit containing a battery and a light bulb. The wire in the light is like a narrow bridge. The electrons lose energy as they cross this bridge.

You can now add a third bulb in series. The electrons have to pass through three lamps, so they are dimmer still. More electrons could be added by adding more batteries to the circuit. The batteries must be connected positive to negative terminal to complete the circuit. Now the bulbs have more electrons and should be brighter.

Remember: there must be a complete circuit for the electrons to flow. Any break in the circuit will prevent the flow of electricity and the bulbs will go out. If a bulb is removed from a series circuit, the other bulbs will fail. Christmas tree lights often work like this.

ACTIVITY

MAKING A SERIES CIRCUIT

> ### YOU NEED
>
> - **2 dry cell batteries in battery holders**
> - **3 bulbs in bulb holders**
> - **a switch**
> - **6 short lengths of insulated copper wire**
> - **a screwdriver**

1 Connect a wire from one positive battery terminal to one side of the switch. Connect another wire from the switch to the bulb holder.

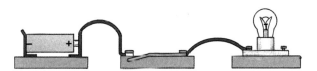

2 Connect the third wire from the bulb holder to the negative battery terminal. You have made a circuit.

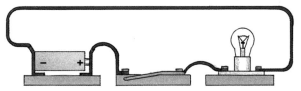

3 Switch on. Does the bulb light? If not, check your circuit.

4 Connect another bulb to the circuit.
5 Switch on. Do both bulbs light?

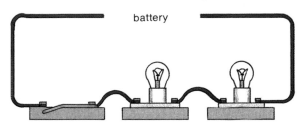

6 Is each bulb as bright as when there was only one bulb in the circuit?
7 Put a third bulb in the circuit. Switch on. What happens?
8 Unscrew one bulb. Switch on. What happens? Why?

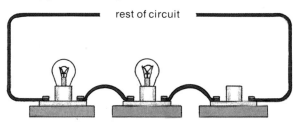

9 Put a second battery into the circuit. Remember to connect the positive terminal of one battery to the negative terminal of the other battery.

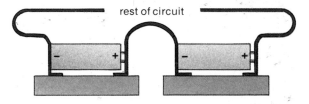

10 Switch on. Are the bulbs brighter now?

TEST YOURSELF

1. How does a switch turn off electricity?
2. Why do bulbs glow more dimly when you add more of them to a series circuit?
3. Draw a series circuit with two batteries and two bulbs in it.

PARALLEL CIRCUITS

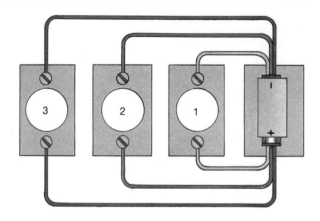

In a series circuit, the light bulbs are placed in a series; that is, they are placed one after the other, like beads in a necklace. The electrons in the circuit have to pass through each bulb before returning to the positive electrode of the battery. If one bulb breaks or fails, the circuit is broken and all the bulbs fail.

However, there is a way to wire a circuit full of bulbs so that one can fail while the others stay alight.

Suppose that you want to wire three bulbs. Bulb 1 is wired to the positive and negative terminals of a battery. So is bulb 2, in a separate little circuit of its own. The same goes for bulb 3. This system of wiring is called a parallel circuit, because each simple circuit is parallel to another. An electron has a choice of little simple circuits to travel through. If it passes down circuit 1, it will light bulb 1, and so on. The current divides equally between all three circuits. If one bulb should fail, it only breaks one of the simple

circuits and that bulb goes out. The other two circuits are still intact and their pathways complete. The other two bulbs will stay alight. It is therefore easy to identify the broken bulb and replace it in a parallel circuit. It is much more difficult to identify in a series circuit; each bulb must be tested in turn.

Attaching more bulbs in parallel to a battery will not dim the bulbs. Each gets the battery's force and lights up brightly.

The national Christmas tree in Washington D.C., USA. The lights are arranged in parallel circuits, so that if one light bulb fails, the others in the display will stay alight.

ACTIVITY

MAKING A PARALLEL CIRCUIT

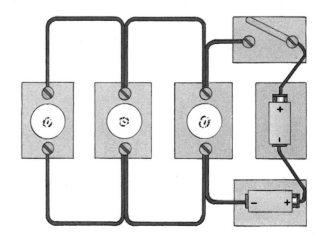

> **YOU NEED**
>
> - **2 batteries and holders**
> - **a switch**
> - **3 bulbs in bulb holders**
> - **a screwdriver**
> - **7 short lengths of insulated copper wire**

1 Put the three bulb holders side by side.
2 Connect together one side of all the bulb holders.
3 Use another two wires to join together the other side of the bulb holders.

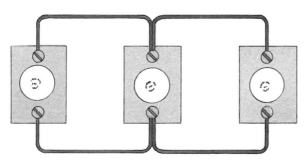

4 Connect a wire from one positive battery terminal to one side of the switch.
5 Connect another wire from the switch to one side of the first bulb holders.
6 Connect the other side of the first bulb holder to the negative battery terminal.

7 Switch on. What happens? Do all the bulbs light?
8 Unscrew one bulb and remove it. Switch on.

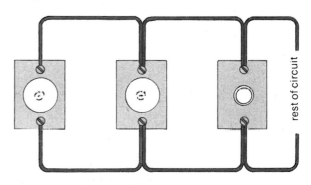

rest of circuit

9 Do the other two bulbs light? What happens to their brightness?
10 Follow the pathway of the electrons from the negative battery terminal around your parallel circuit.
11 Switch off.
12 Repeat your experiment by unscrewing another bulb. What happens?

TEST YOURSELF

1. What is an advantage of a parallel electric circuit compared to a series electric circuit?
2. Draw a diagram of a parallel electric circuit that uses a battery, a switch and three bulbs.
3. Describe how a parallel circuit works.

CONDUCTORS AND INSULATORS

These wires are insulated with a poor conductor, so that they do not pass electricity to one another.

Electrical energy is like heat energy; it travels better through some materials than through others. Where it travels easily, the material is called a good conductor. Metals are good conductors of electricity. These materials contain electrons that can move about more easily than in bad conductors. Normally, these electrons move about the conductor in a random way.

If you connect one end of a good conductor to the negative terminal of a battery and the other end to an electric circuit, electricity will flow along the conductor. You have made a pathway for the electrons to flow from the negative terminal of the battery to the positive terminal.

The difference in the number of electrons at one end compared with the other end is called the potential difference. This is measured in volts.

A bad conductor is called an insulator. An insulator has few mobile electrons. When an insulator is connected to a battery, there are not enough electrons in the insulator able to move to give an electric current. As no current is formed, no electricity passes.

Insulators, therefore, act as a barrier to electricity. Copper is a good conductor; rubber is a good insulator. If copper wire is covered with rubber, the electrons will stay in the copper and go around the circuit. The rubber stops them 'leaking' away.

ACTIVITY

MAKING A CONDUCTIVITY BOARD

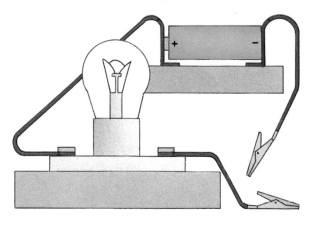

YOU NEED

- **a battery**
- **a bulb and bulb holder**
- **2 crocodile clips**
- **a block of soft wood**
- **a screwdriver**
- **3 short lengths of insulated wire**
- **objects to be tested:**
  e.g. glass slide, rubber,
  plastic, copper wire, iron nail,
  brass screw, pencil, wood

1 Connect one wire to the negative
battery terminal and the 2 other wires
to either side of the bulb holder.

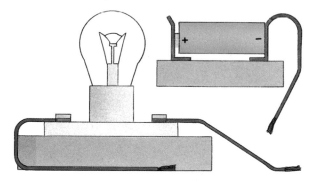

2 Connect one side of the bulb holder to
the positive battery terminal.
3 Connect a crocodile clip to both free
ends of wire.

4 Clip the two ends of the wire with the
crocodile clips. What happens?

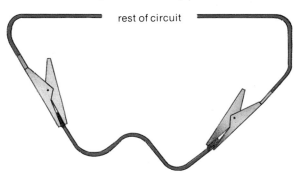

rest of circuit

5 Notice that the copper wire conducts
electricity, completing the circuit. The
copper is therefore a good conductor.
Record your result.
6 Fix the plastic between the clips.
Does the bulb light? If not, the plastic
is an insulator.
7 Try all kinds of materials to see if they
are conductors or insulators. Record
your results.
8 Sharpen both ends of a pencil. Is
pencil 'lead' a good conductor?

TEST YOURSELF

1. What is the potential difference in a circuit?
2. Explain how a good conductor conducts electricity in an electrical circuit.
3. Describe how you would test a material to see whether it is a conductor or
an insulator.

ELECTRICAL RESISTANCE

Good conductors of electricity have lots of mobile electrons in them and so they allow electrons from a battery to pass easily through them. As the electrons move along, they will collide with atoms in the conductor and this slows down the electrons. This slowing down of the electrons is called the resistance of the conductor.

All conducting wires have a resistance, as they are all made of atoms that the electrons can collide with. The longer the piece of wire, the more atoms there are for the electrons to bump into and be slowed down by. So, the longer the wire, the higher its resistance. That is why, in experiments using circuits, we try to use short wire to cut down resistance.

Thick wire has a lower resistance than thin wire. In thick wire, there is a wider surface area for the electrons to pass through, which gives more room for them to avoid collision with atoms. A thin wire has a greater resistance than thick wire.

We measure resistance in ohms, named after the German scientist Georg Simon Ohm, who worked on resistance in the nineteenth century. He stated 'Ohm's Law', which says that the resistance (R) of an electrical circuit is the number of volts in the circuit (V) divided by the current, measured in amps:

$$R = V \div I \text{ (current)}$$

Same thickness but different length:

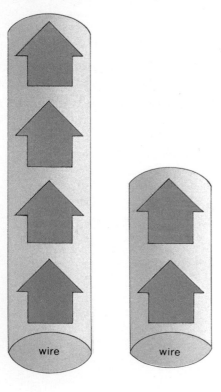

Same length but different thickness:

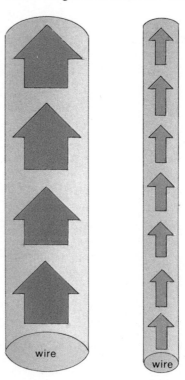

ACTIVITY

VARIABLE RESISTORS

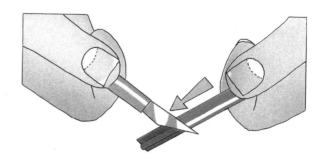

YOU NEED

- **a collection of pencils of differing hardness**
- **a battery**
- **a bulb and bulb holder**
- **a screwdriver**
- **5 short lengths of insulated wire**
- **a small saw**
- **a sharp knife**

WARNING: be very careful when using a saw or a knife.

1 Set up the circuit as you did on page 25.

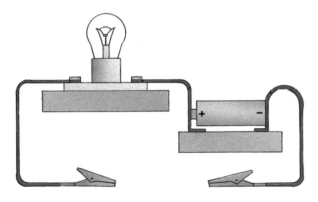

2 Use the saw to cut the pencils to the same length.
3 Carefully cut away all the wood from one side of the pencil until you have exposed the pencil 'lead'.

4 Notice that the darkest pencil 'lead' is the softest.
5 Soft pencil 'leads' are almost all graphite. To make a pencil hard, this is mixed with clay. Graphite is a form of carbon that conducts electricity.
6 Test the conductivity of each pencil.

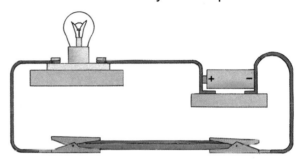

7 Compare the brightness of the bulb to the pencil hardness.
8 You should find that the harder the pencil, the higher its resistance.
9 Bring the clips closer together while they are touching the pencil 'lead'. What happens to the light?

Variable resistors control the amount of electricity passing through them. Variable resistors are used as light dimmers and volume controls on radio and television.

TEST YOURSELF

1. What is the difference between hard and soft pencils?
2. What does a resistor do in an electrical circuit?
3. Name two uses for a variable resistor.

HEAT FROM ELECTRICITY

This electric bar heater has coils of wire with a naturally high resistance.

One of the main uses of electrical energy is to convert it into heat energy. We use this in electric fires, fan heaters, electric irons, kettles and electric stoves. Can you think of other machines that use electricity to give heat?

All these devices work because of electrical resistance. When electrons pass down a wire, they collide into the atoms. The more atoms with which they collide, the greater the resistance. When the electrons collide with the atoms, they make them vibrate. These vibrating atoms are hit by more electrons, causing them to vibrate more and more, and the material gets hotter and hotter. In order to get the maximum number of collisions, we first use a wire that has a naturally high resistance, such as nickel-chrome wire. We then make this wire very thin. Thin wire increases the resistance

because it acts as a narrow bridge to the passage of the electrons, so increasing collisions.

The hot wire can weaken, so we usually wrap it around a china-like substance that will heat up as well and give out heat like the hot bricks in a storage heater.

Obviously, the more electric power provided, the more electrons there are to collide with the atoms to generate heat. We measure this electric power in watts (W), named after James Watt, who invented the steam engine. In electricity, watts are volts multiplied by amps:

$$P \text{ (power in watts)} = V \times I \text{ (current)}$$

Most electric fires are measured in kilowatts, or 1000 watts.

ACTIVITY

HEAT FROM ELECTRIC POWER

YOU NEED

- **a battery**
- **a bulb in a bulb holder**
- **a screwdriver**
- **a switch**
- **sticky tape**
- **a thermometer**
- **a styrofoam cup with a small quantity of water**
- **3 lengths of insulated copper wire**

1 Connect together the battery, switch and bulb.

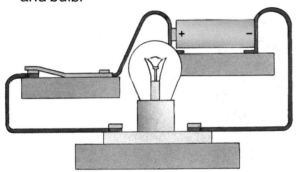

2 Switch on. Does the bulb light? Switch off.
3 Place the bulb in the styrofoam cup, so that the glass of the bulb is under water.
4 *Make sure that only the glass of the bulb is in the water.*

5 Tape the wires to the cup to hold the bulb in place.

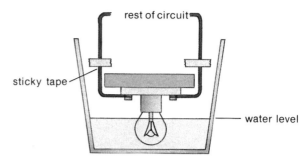

6 Use the thermometer to test the temperature of the water.
7 Record this temperature.
8 Switch on and leave the bulb alight in the water for five minutes.

Temperature of water before switching on (°C)	
Temperature of water after 5 minutes (°C)	
Temperature of water after 10 minutes (°C)	

9 Record the temperature of the water. How much has the temperature increased?
10 What happens if you leave the bulb alight for ten minutes?
11 What happens if you use two bulbs?

Remember: for the best results, you need the smallest amount of water.

TEST YOURSELF

1. Name three pieces of equipment that convert electrical energy into heat energy.
2. Explain how an electric fire works.
3. How do we calculate the electrical power of a heating appliance such as an electric fire?

LIGHT FROM ELECTRICITY

If you look at any electric light bulb, you will see that the filament that glows is very thin. This filament is rather like the element in an electric fire. The filament is a fine coil of wire that has a high resistance. The wire usually chosen is made of tungsten, because it can get white hot and still not melt. Tungsten wire has a high resistance.

In order for the tungsten wire to glow white hot, it must be very long and very thin. To get this long length of wire into a light bulb, the wire is coiled around to form a tight coil and then this coil is loosely coiled again.

The wire coil is long, thin and heavy, so it has to be supported by stronger wires.

If the bulb were full of air, the oxygen in the air would combine with the tungsten when it became hot and would burn up instantly. For this reason, all air is taken out of the bulb and the bulb is refilled with a harmless, inactive gas called argon.

Like the electric fire, the power of the light bulb is written on the glass bulb. The power is measured in watts (see page 28). Most household bulbs are 40 W (dimmest), 60 W, 75 W, 100 W or 150 W (brightest).

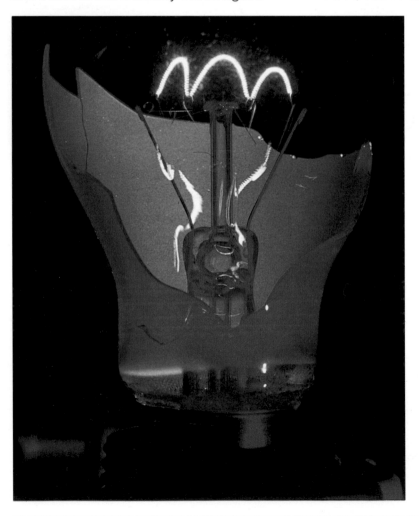

This is an ordinary household bulb. The filament, or fine wire coil, is made of a metal called tungsten, which has a high resistance. It is very thin, and glows as it is heated up by the efforts of the electrons to pass through it.

ACTIVITY

LOOKING AT BULBS

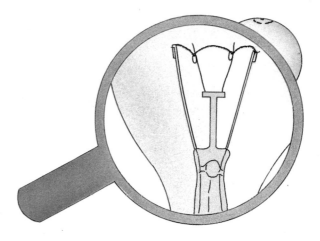

> **YOU NEED**
>
> • **a collection of light bulbs, including torch bulbs and various clear household table-lamp bulbs**
> • **a magnifying lens**

1 Look at a clear table-lamp bulb. What wattage is this bulb? What does this tell you?

2 How does the bulb fit into its socket?
3 Look at the fitting end of the bulb. What is it made of? Where does the electricity enter the bulb?
4 Notice how the electric wires are separated by the glass stem.
5 Look through a lens at the tungsten coil. See how it is coiled and looped.

6 How is it supported? Notice how the coil moves gently within the supports.
7 Will this bulb work or not? Look at the coil. Is it intact or broken?

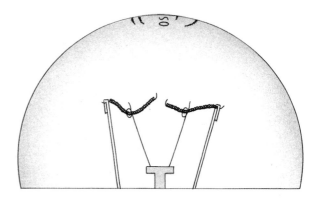

8 Compare this bulb with other household table-lamp bulbs. Draw what you see. Label the parts.
9 Compare a table-lamp bulb with a torch bulb. What are the differences?
10 Draw a torch bulb.
11 Arrange your bulbs in order of brightness. How will you do this without switching them on?

TEST YOURSELF

1. What is the wire in a table-lamp bulb made of?
2. Why is a table-lamp bulb full of argon gas?
3. Explain how electric power is turned into light power.

FUSES

The dry-cell batteries that we use give less than one amp of electricity and are quite safe. Household electricity is much more dangerous, as it has to heat cookers, fires and work other appliances.

If too much current flows into an appliance, the electrons could 'leak away' in large numbers. If you come into contact with current leaks, you can be killed by an electric shock. Also, the appliance could catch fire, or be ruined in some other way. To prevent this happening, each circuit in the house, and every appliance, has a control to regulate the amount of electricity. These controls are called fuses.

A fuse works by resistance. If the correct amount of electricity passes in the circuit, the fuse stays as a wire, allowing the circuit to work. If too much electricity passes due to a fault in the wire or an appliance, the fuse heats up because it is a resistor. It heats up quickly and melts, breaking the circuit. No more electricity will pass until the fault is repaired. If you do not repair the fault, but just replace the fuse with a new one, this fuse will also melt, cutting off the electricity again.

The sort of fuse that you may have seen is probably a cartridge. Inside the glass case of the cartridge is the fuse wire. Fuses are of different sizes, depending on the amount of electricity they will allow to pass before melting.

Cartridge fuses used in a car.

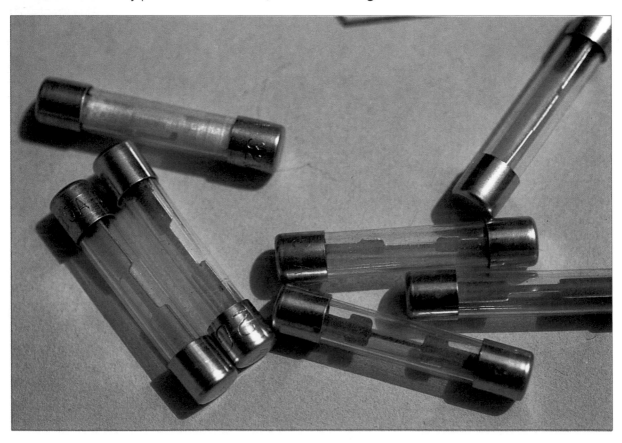

ACTIVITY

YOU NEED

- **steel wool**
- **a battery**
- **a wood block**
- **2 crocodile clips**
- **a switch**
- **a screwdriver**
- **3 short lengths of insulated copper wire**
- **a collection of cartridge fuses**
- **a magnifying lens**

1 Use the insulated wire to connect one clip to one battery terminal.
2 Use another length of wire to connect the other battery terminal to one side of the switch.
3 Connect the other side of the switch to the clip.

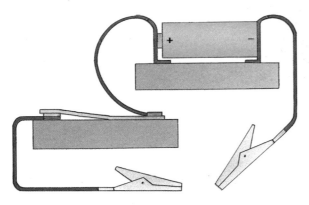

4 Sort out your steel wool. Select a strand.

5 Put this strand of steel wool onto the wood block.
6 Check that the switch is off.
7 Use clips to grip each end of the strand of steel wool.

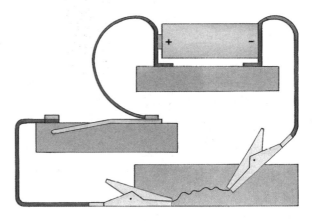

8 Switch on. What happens to the steel wool?
9 You may need two batteries in the circuit if you have trouble with your fuse.
10 Do not repeat this experiment too many times as it drains the battery.
11 Look at your collection of fuses through a magnifying lens.
12 Look at a 3 amp, 5 amp and 13 amp fuse. What is the difference between the thickness of the wire? Why?
13 Are all the fuses intact, or have some been 'blown'?

> WARNING: this experiment could be dangerous. Get an adult to help you.

TEST YOURSELF

1. What does a fuse do?
2. Why should you always have the correct fuse fitted, as written on the appliance?
3. Explain how a fuse works.

WATER CONDUCTS ELECTRICITY

Electrolysis (destroying by electricity) of a metal in a conducting solution, such as salt water. This is part of an electrical circuit, which will only work if the metal is dipped into the solution. The electricity breaks down the water, producing bubbles of hydrogen, which is one of the elements that makes the substance water. The metal gradually dissolves as more electricity passes.

To be able to conduct electricity, a material must be a good conductor (see page 24). A good conductor has lots of mobile electrons.

Pure water does not have any mobile electrons, so it is an insulator, as there are no electrons present to form an electric current.

If table salt is dissolved in water, this changes. Table salt is a chemical called sodium chloride. When sodium chloride dissolves in water it ionizes. That means that it splits into ions, which are electrically charged particles. There are sodium ions (positive) and chloride ions (negative) in the water. The word ion comes from the Greek word meaning wanderer. It describes the way in which these ions move freely in the water.

The chloride ions with their negative charges can act just like electrons and carry electricity through the water. The more ions in the water, the more charges there are present, so more electricity can flow. Most water has some chemicals dissolved in it. All dissolved chemicals ionize. Tap water has chemicals dissolved in it, so it conducts electricity. Because of this, never use any electrical appliance near water. Never touch an electrical plug, or any electrical appliance, with wet hands or the electricity will go through you, giving an electric shock that could kill. Your hands can also conduct electricity if they are sweaty, because sweat contains salt.

ACTIVITY

YOU NEED

- **a battery**
- **a bulb in a bulb holder**
- **a screwdriver**
- **3 short lengths of insulated copper wire**
- **a jar**
- **a spoon**
- **pure (distilled) water**
- **tap water**
- **salt**

1 Connect one battery terminal to one side of the bulb holder.
2 Connect a wire to the other side of the bulb holder and place it in the empty jar.
3 Connect a wire to the other battery terminal and place that wire in the jar.

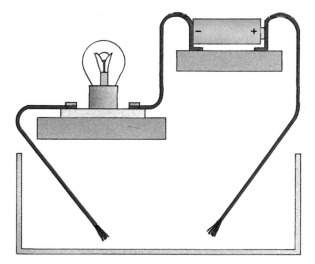

4 Touch together the two wires in the jar.
5 You have now made a circuit and the bulb should light.
6 Separate the wires in the jar. The bulb will go out.
7 Half fill the jar with pure distilled water.
8 Check that the ends of the wires are covered by the water.

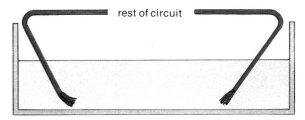

9 Does the bulb light? Is electricity passing through the water? Is pure water an insulator or a conductor?
10 Empty out the pure water.
11 Replace it with tap water. Does the bulb light?
12 Bring the wires closer together. What happens?
13 Stir some salt into the water. Does salt water conduct electricity?

14 Slowly move the wires apart. What happens?
15 Stir in a little more salt. What happens?

TEST YOURSELF

1. Is pure water a good conductor or an insulator? Why?
2. What happens to salt when it is dissolved in water?
3. Why must you never touch electrical appliances with wet hands?

ELECTROPLATING

Steel is a strong metal and is used to make many things. Unfortunately, steel rusts. You can prevent rusting by covering the steel with something to protect it. You can paint the steel, or you can coat parts of the steel with chromium. When the steel on cars is covered with chromium we use the term 'chromium plated', which means electroplated with chromium.

Expensive spoons are made of silver and hallmarked to show this. Some spoons have EPNS stamped on them. This means electroplated nickel silver. It has only a fine coat of silver on it, although it looks like a silver spoon.

To electroplate a spoon with silver, the chemical silver nitrate must be dissolved in water. Silver nitrate, when it dissolves in water, will split up into silver ions (positive) and nitrate ions (negative). A spoon is then connected to the negative terminal of the battery and so becomes the negative electrode, which we call the cathode. A bar of silver is attached to the positive terminal of the battery and becomes the positive electrode or anode. As the electric current passes, the positive silver ions in the water are attracted to the negative (cathode) spoon and stick to it. The negative nitrate ions are attracted to the positive electrode, which is the bar of silver. The nitrate ions cause the silver on the bar to dissolve, making more silver ions. This goes on until the spoon is smoothly plated with silver. You will notice that the silver bar is 'used up' in this process.

Electroplating a nickel spoon. The silver anode dissolves to form silver ions, which move to the nickel cathode and become silver metal again.

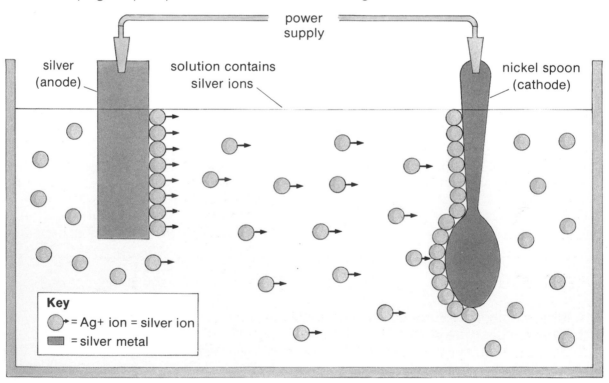

ACTIVITY

ELECTROPLATING WITH COPPER

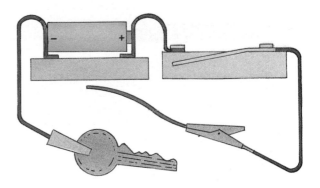

> **YOU NEED**
>
> - **object to be plated: e.g. brass key**
> - **a bar of copper**
> - **a battery**
> - **a switch**
> - **sticky tape**
> - **an empty milk carton**
> - **salt**
> - **a bottle of white vinegar**
> - **3 short lengths of insulated wire**
> - **2 crocodile clips**

6 Connect the switch to the copper, using a crocodile clip and a wire.

7 Place the copper bar and key in the tank until they are mostly covered by the vinegar, but do not let the clips dip in.

8 Tape the wires to the side of the carton with sticky tape.

1 Cut a clean milk carton in half.

2 Half fill the carton with white vinegar.

3 Stir salt into the vinegar until no more will dissolve.

level of vinegar

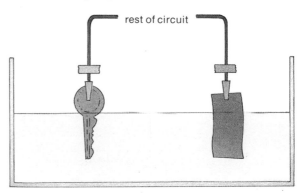

rest of circuit

4 Connect the brass key to be plated to the negative battery terminal, using a crocodile clip and wire.

5 Connect the positive battery terminal to a switch.

9 Switch on. What changes do you notice on the key?

10 Are bubbles being formed? If bubbles stick to the key, shake them off.

11 How long does it take for the key to be covered in copper?

12 Look at the copper bar. What is happening to it?

> ## TEST YOURSELF
>
> **1.** What is a negative electrode called? What is a positive electrode called?
>
> **2.** When silver nitrate ionizes in water, which is the positive ion?
>
> **3.** Describe how you could electroplate a spoon.

STORING ELECTRICITY

Left *A spark plug from a car, showing the electric arc (spark) that must be made at regular intervals, so that the car will run smoothly.*

Below *A diagram of a lead-acid battery (accumulator), the type used in cars.*

Cars, when they are moving, use most of their energy to generate electricity. Cars do this by using an alternator, which is similar to a dynamo (see page 44). Cars need to generate electricity to work the lights and other electrical parts of the car. They also need to be able to store electricity, so that there is power to move the starter motor to turn over the engine and start the car.

The car battery is an accumulator (storer of electrical energy) as well as a battery (provider of electrical energy). Car batteries are often lead-acid cell batteries. The first lead-acid cell batteries were invented in 1881, and were important in the development of the first cars.

A lead-acid cell battery consists of a series of cells. Each cell consists of plates of lead immersed in dilute acid. When the car is going, electricity passes to the lead-acid cells for storing. There are lead plates at the positive and negative terminals acting as electrodes. Some lead cells are cathodes and some are anodes. The positive plate (the anode) becomes coated with lead oxide. The negative plate (the cathode) stays as lead.

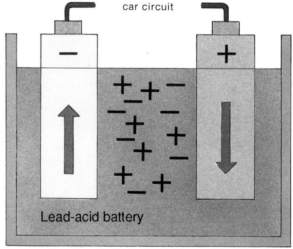

car circuit

Lead-acid battery

When the engine is switched off, no more lead oxide forms and the electrical energy is stored. The car needs electrical energy to start, and when the ignition key is turned, the lead oxide on the anode starts to combine with the acid to form lead sulphate and water. This continues until no lead oxide is left and the battery is 'flat'. When the battery is charged again with electricity, the lead sulphate is turned back to lead oxide and acid, and electricity is stored.

ACTITIVY

STORING ELECTRICITY IN A LEAD-ACID CELL

YOU NEED

- **2 good strong dry-cell batteries (6V)**
- **2 small strips of lead**
- **sodium sulphate (Glauber's salt)**
- **a glass jar**
- **2 short lengths of insulated copper wire**
- **sticky tape**
- **a bulb and bulb holder**
- **a screwdriver**

1 Make a strong solution of sodium sulphate by dissolving it in warm water.
2 Half fill the jar with it.
3 Fix both strips of lead to a length of covered copper wire. Make sure there is a good connection. Tape the wires to the lead.

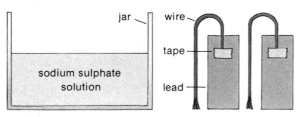

4 Connect the other end of the wires, one to the positive terminal of one battery, the other to the negative terminal of the other battery.

5 Connect the batteries together in series.
6 Put both strips of lead into the sodium sulphate solution. Make sure that the lead strips do not touch.

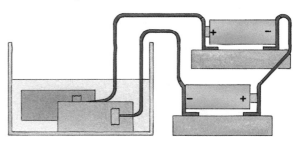

7 What happens to your storage cell?
8 Do bubbles appear on your lead strips?
9 Does the positive lead strip, the anode, change colour?
10 After five minutes, your lead-acid cell should be charged.
11 Disconnect both batteries.
12 Carefully connect the wires from your storage cell to a bulb in a bulb holder.

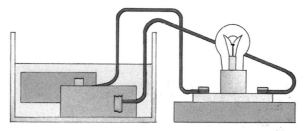

13 Does your bulb light?
14 Notice how your storage cell soon becomes drained.

TEST YOURSELF

1. What does a car battery do?
2. Explain what happens when electricity is fed into a lead-acid cell.
3. Explain what happens when a lead-acid cell acts as a battery to provide electricity.

ELECTRICITY MAKES MAGNETISM

When electrons flow through a wire, making an electric current, a magnetic field is created around the wire. This magnetic field, or magnetism, is created as a magnetic force spiralling around the wire. The magnetism is created clockwise around the wire, in the direction of the electric current.

A magnetic compass needle usually points north because the magnetized needle of the compass is attracted to the Earth's magnetic north pole. If a magnetized compass needle is placed near a copper wire the compass needle will continue to point north, because copper is not a magnetic metal and so will not affect the compass needle. When the electric current is switched on, the magnetic field that is made will immediately affect the compass needle. The direction of the flow of electricity will decide whether the magnetic field created near the magnetized compass

needle is north or south. If it is a south field, the compass needle will be strongly attracted. If it is a north field, the needle will be strongly repelled.

The strength of the magnetic field created depends on the number of electrons flowing through the wire. Therefore, the more electricity flowing through the wire, the greater the magnetic field around the wire.

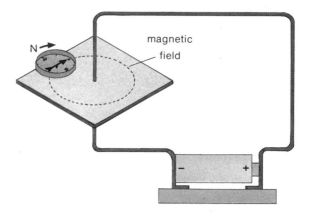

Below *A small magnet hovers above a piece of superconductor. The electricity in the superconductor creates a magnetic field, which repels the other magnet.*

Above *A diagram to show the effect of a wire carrying electricity on a magnetic compass. The electricity in the wire creates a magnetic field around it.*

ACTIVITY

YOU NEED

- **a magnetic compass**
- **a bulb in a bulb holder**
- **a 6V battery**
- **a switch**
- **a small cardboard or plastic box**
- **a screwdriver**
- **insulated copper wire**

1 Make a circuit using the battery, switch and bulb holder. Switch on.
2 Does the bulb light? Switch off.
3 Place the compass on the wire. Check that the compass needle points north.
4 Move the wire so that it also points north-south, in line with the needle.

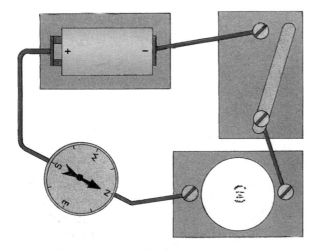

5 Switch on. Does the bulb light? What happens to the compass needle when electricity flows through the wire?
6 Switch off. What happens?
7 Try this with the battery connected the other way around.

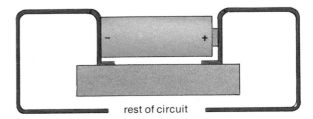

rest of circuit

8 Place the compass in the box.
9 Wind the copper wire 10 times around the box.

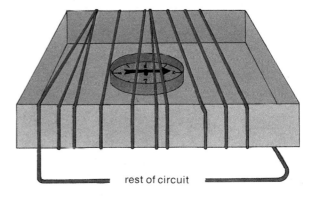

rest of circuit

10 Switch on. Does the compass needle move more than before?
11 Wind the copper wire 20 times around the box. Does the compass needle react more or less?
12 Does the number of turns of wire increase the magnetic effect?

TEST YOURSELF

1. Describe how you would prove that a magnetic field is created when electrons flow through a wire.
2. When electricity flows through a wire, where is the magnetic field created?
3. Explain how the number of turns in a coil of wire affects the amount of magnetism created.

ELECTRIC MOTORS

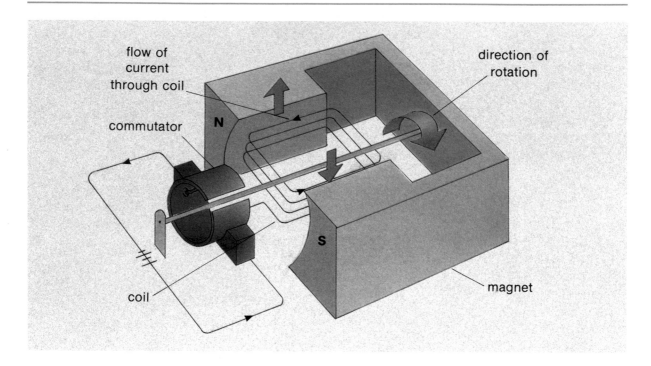

flow of current through coil

commutator

coil

N

S

direction of rotation

magnet

You have found out that electricity and magnetism are closely linked and can have an effect on one another. This is put to good use in electric motors, where electrical energy is turned into mechanical (movement) energy.

An electric motor consists of a coil of wire held in a magnetic field from a permanent magnet. A flow of electrons (current) is sent through the coil. The magnet affects the moving electrons and the coil turns. This is because the current makes a magnetic field around the wire. The current is sent through in such a way that to start with, the north pole of the magnet lines up with the north pole of the magnetic field around the wire. The two repel each other, and this causes the coil to turn. It tries to line itself up with unlike poles together.

Just before the coil lines up north-south with the magnet and gets fixed in position, the flow of electricity is sent the other way.

A diagram to show the main parts of a simple electric motor.

Now the north pole of the coil has become its south pole (see page 40). However, it is turning so that the south of the magnet will now meet the new south of the coil. They repel each other at this side, and the coil carries on turning.

Once again, just before the unlike poles line up, the current is reversed. This carries on, and the coil keeps on turning. The spinning coil can be used to turn other components attached to the motor.

The current that changes direction every half-turn is called an alternating current (a.c.). In Britain the household mains current is a.c. If the current comes from a battery and flows only in one direction (direct current or d.c.), the motor has a special attachment inside it called a commutator, which reverses the current when necessary.

ACTIVITY

YOU NEED

- **an electric motor and the battery that works it**
- **a switch**
- **a crocodile clip**
- **a new pencil**
- **4 short lengths of insulated copper wire**
- **a screwdriver**
- **a sharp knife**

1 Make a circuit by connecting together the battery switch and motor. Switch on.

2 Does the electric motor turn?

3 Disconnect your circuit.

4 Fasten a crocodile clip to one end of a length of insulated wire.

5 Connect the other end to the negative battery terminal.

6 Connect one wire from the positive battery terminal to one side of the switch.

7 Connect the other side of the switch to one side of the motor.

8 Connect a wire to the other side of the motor.

9 Use a crocodile clip to grip this wire. Switch on.

10 Is your circuit complete? Does the motor turn? Switch off.

11 Sharpen one end of the pencil. Using the knife carefully, cut away all the pencil wood from one side of the pencil until you have exposed all the pencil lead.

12 Use the clip to grip the pointed end of the pencil lead. Switch on.

13 Touch the loose wire to the middle of the pencil lead. Does the motor turn?

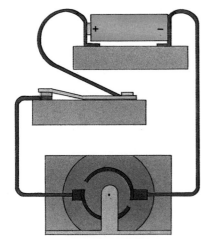

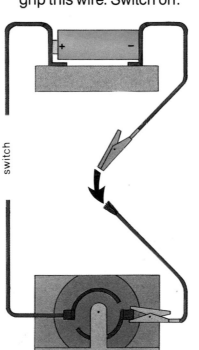

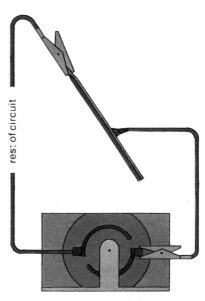

14 Move this wire up and down the pencil lead. Notice how you control the motor.

TEST YOURSELF

1. Name three things that use an electric motor.

2. Why is magnetism important for an electric motor to work?

3. Describe how an electric motor works.

GENERATING ELECTRICITY

Electricity will drive an electric motor, in which electrical energy is converted into mechanical energy. If mechanical energy is used to turn a coil between a magnetic field, electricity is made. An electric motor used to create electricity in this way is called a dynamo. The generator in a power station is a dynamo. First, you need power to turn the dynamo. Sometimes, steam power is used, or falling water, as in hydroelectric power. When steam is used, it is made by burning coal, or oil, or using nuclear power to heat water to create the steam. The steam or the falling water turns the blades of a turbine, which in turn drives the dynamo. The electricity made then passes through a transformer to increase its voltage.

The electricity produced in Britain is at 132,000 volts and travels along wires strung between great pylons. This electricity is alternating current (a.c.). A dry-cell battery produces direct current (d.c.). It only flows in one direction. Alternating current changes direction 100 times a second, called 50 cycles. Sending electricity as alternating current at this high voltage means that there is less power loss due to heat. This can happen when the electricity is sent over great distances. Of course, these wires need massive insulators. This electricity is too powerful for our homes, so it is reduced by transformers in transformer stations (or substations). The power of household electricity varies in different countries. In Britain and Australia, for example, it is reduced to 240 volts, while in Canada it is reduced to 110 volts.

In towns, this electricity enters our homes through underground cables, but in rural areas, it may come through overhead wires.

Very thick insulating material is used to isolate the cables that carry electricity at very high voltages across the country. If such isolators were not used, the cables would pass their electricity to one another, and cause widespread power cuts.

ACTIVITIES

RESEARCH INTO ELECTRIC POWER GENERATORS

> YOU NEED • **access to a library**

1 Find out about steam generators.
2 Look at cost and safety. What are the advantages of generating steam using coal, oil or nuclear power?

What are the disadvantages?
3 Find out about hydroelectric power, wind power, solar power, wave and tide power and other alternative energy sources.
4 Mount a display of this research.

MAKING ELECTRICITY

> YOU NEED
>
> • **a strong bar magnet**
> • **a magnetic compass**
> • **a long length of fine insulated wire**
> • **a broom handle**
> • **a cardboard or plastic box**

1 Put the compass in the box.
2 Wind 20 turns of wire around the box.
3 Make a 50-turn coil at the other end of the wire by winding it around a broom handle.

4 Check that the coil is well away from the compass.
5 Slowly put the north pole of your bar magnet into the 50-turn coil. What happens to the compass needle?

6 If the needle moves there must be electricity in the wire. Slowly withdraw the magnet. What happens?
7 Slowly put the south pole of the magnet into the coil. Which way does the needle point? What does that tell you?
8 How could you make a stronger electric current in the coil?

TEST YOURSELF

1. Name three ways in which an electrical generating power station is fuelled.
2. Why is electricity sent across country at such a high voltage?
3. What is a dynamo and how does it work?

Glossary

Alternating current (a.c.) An electric current that flows first in one direction, then in the opposite. The direction changes at regular intervals.

Appliance A piece of equipment that is worked by electricity.

Attraction In electricity, the power or force that pulls two unlike charges together. In magnetism, the power or force that pulls two unlike poles together.

Carbon An element found in all living things, as well as in graphite, diamond and coal.

Conductor In electricity, a substance through which electrons flow easily. Very good conductors have a low electrical resistance.

Current The flow of electrons through a conductor. It is measured in amperes (amps).

Direct current (d.c.) An electric current that flows in one direction only.

Electrode A conductor through which electric current enters or leaves a battery or electrolyte.

Electrolyte Usually, a solution or liquid that conducts electricity. However, electrolytes do have other forms: for example, a paste-like substance inside dry-cell batteries. The difference between an electrolyte and a conductor such as a metal is that the electrolyte contains ions to carry the charge. In a conductor, electrons move.

Electron A negatively charged particle present in all atoms. Free electrons are responsible for electrical conduction in most materials.

Electroplating A method of coating one metal with another, usually by passing an electric current through a special circuit. This contains the metal to be coated as one electrode and the metal for coating as the other electrode, and the conducting solution between the two.

Filament A very thin thread.

Insulator A material that is a very bad conductor: e.g., plastic, rubber, wood.

Mobile Easily able to move or be moved.

Ohm The unit used to measure electrical resistance.

Potential difference Potential difference is the difference in electrical force between 2 terminals.

Power The rate at which work is done, or energy is used. Electrical power is measured in watts.

Proton A positively charged particle that is found in the nucleus of every atom. Its charge exactly balances that of one electron.

Pylon In electricity, a tall steel tower that carries electrical wires.

Repel To push away from. In electricity, the effect of two like charges on each other. In magnetism, the effect of two like poles on each other (repulsion).

Resistance In electricity, the ability of a substance to conduct electricity. The higher the resistance, the less current passes through. It is measured in ohms.

Transformer A device that alters the voltage of an electric current, either increasing or decreasing it.

Turbine A revolving motor in which a wheel with blades is driven by a liquid or gas passing through it.

Books to read

Discovering Electricity Neil Ardley (Franklin Watts, 1984)
Electricity C. L. Boltz (Faber, 1985)
Electricity Alan Cooper (Macdonald, 1983)
Focus on Electricity Mark Lambert (Wayland, 1988)
Electricity and Magnetism Kathryn Whyman (Franklin Watts, 1986)

Picture acknowledgements

The author and publishers would like to thank the following for allowing illustrations to be reproduced in this book: PHOTRI 32; Science Photo Library 6, 18, 24, 30, 38, 40; Topham Picture Library 28; ZEFA *cover*, 8, 22, 34, 44. All artwork is by Marilyn Clay. Cover artwork by Jenny Hughes.

Index

Accumulator 38
Alternating current
    (a.c.) 42, 44
Alternator 38
Ampère, A.M. 18
Amps 26, 28, 32, 33
Anode 36
Atoms 8, 26, 28
Attraction (attract) 11, 12
Australia 44

Canada 44
Cathode 36, 38
Commutator 42
Conductors 24–25, 26,
    32, 34, 35
Current 14, 16, 18, 20, 22,
    24, 26, 28, 34, 40, 42, 45

Dimmers 26
Direct current (d.c.) 42, 44
Dynamo 30, 44

Electricity meter 14, 15
Electric shock 6, 16, 32, 34
Electrodes 16, 18, 22, 36,
    38
Electrolyte 16, 18
Electrons 8, 10, 12, 14, 16,
    18, 19, 20, 22, 24, 26, 28,
    34, 40, 42
Electroplating 36–37
Electroscope 12–13

Franklin, Benjamin 6
Fuses 32-33

Generators 44–45

Heat 14, 15, 24, 28, 44

Ions 34, 36
Insulators 24–25, 34, 35,
    44

Lead-acid batteries 38
Light 14, 15, 20
Lightning 6, 10–11
Lightning conductors 10

Magnetism 40–41, 42
Metal 6, 10, 14, 36, 40
Motors 14, 15, 42–43, 44

Negative charges 6, 8, 10,
    12, 13, 14, 34
Neutrons 8

Ohm, Georg Simon 26
Ohm's Law 26

Positive charges 6, 8, 10,
    12, 16
Potential difference 24
Power stations 14
Protons 8
Pylons 44

Repulsion (repel) 11, 12
Resistance 26–27, 28,
    30, 32

Static electricity 6–7, 8–9,
    10, 12–13, 14
Sound 14, 15

Thunder 10
Transformer 44
Turbine 44

Variable resistors 26
Volta, Alessandro 18
Voltage 15, 18, 44
Volume controls 26

Watt, James 28